In loving memory of
Emma Charlotte young
from
The Director and Staff of
The Brumback Library

What Happens in Spring?

Weather in Spring

by Jenny Fretland VanVoorst

Bullfrog Books

Ideas for Parents and Teachers

Bullfrog Books let children practice reading informational text at the earliest reading levels. Repetition, familiar words, and photo labels support early readers.

Before Reading

- Discuss the cover photo. What does it tell them?

- Look at the picture glossary together. Read and discuss the words.

Read the Book

- "Walk" through the book and look at the photos. Let the child ask questions. Point out the photo labels.

- Read the book to the child, or have him or her read independently.

After Reading

- Prompt the child to think more. Ask: What is spring weather like where you live? What do you wear outside in the spring?

Bullfrog Books are published by Jump!
5357 Penn Avenue South
Minneapolis, MN 55419
www.jumplibrary.com

Library of Congress Cataloging-in-Publication Data

Fretland VanVoorst, Jenny, 1972– author.
  Weather in spring / by Jenny Fretland VanVoorst.
    pages cm.—(What happens in spring?)
  "Bullfrog Books are published by Jump!."
Audience: Ages 5–8.
Audience: K to grade 3.
  Includes index.
ISBN 978-1-62031-238-4 (hardcover: alk. paper)
ISBN 978-1-62496-325-4 (ebook)
1. Spring—Juvenile literature.
2. Weather—Juvenile literature. I. Title.
QB637.5.F74 2015
 508.2—dc23
                                          2014044467

Series Designer: Ellen Huber
Book Designer: Lindaanne Donohoe

Photo Credits: All photos by Shutterstock except: iStock, 14–14, 16–17, 23br; ThinkStock, 3, 18, 19, 20–21, 22tl, 22bl, 22br, 24.

Printed in the United States of America at Corporate Graphics in North Mankato, Minnesota.

Table of Contents

Warming Up

The sun comes out.

The snow melts.

Goodbye, winter.
Spring is here.

Spring is a time of change.

It is a time of growth.

The sun warms the soil.

Plants poke through
the dirt.

Birds return from the South.

Animals come out
of their burrows.

9

People come
outside too.

Ben rides his bike.

He does not
need a coat.

Spring also
means rain.

Rain makes the
plants grow.

Lia plays in the rain.

She stomps in
the puddles.

Spring can be windy.

Kelly flies a kite.

Whee!

The air gets even warmer.

Baby animals are born.

18

Flowers bloom.

Soon it will be summer!

Kinds of Spring Weather

windy

sunny

rainy

cloudy

Picture Glossary

bloom
When a plant blooms, its flowers open up.

South
The warm part of the world where some birds spend the winter.

burrow
An animal's underground home.

stomp
To step heavily.

Index

To Learn More

Learning more is as easy as 1, 2, 3.

1) Go to www.factsurfer.com

2) Enter "weatherinspring" into the search box.

3) Click the "Surf" button to see a list of websites.

With factsurfer.com, finding more information is just a click away.